A PROCESSION OF WORDS

A Procession of Words *Previously published by*
Minerva Press, London SW7 2JE
under ISBN number 1-85863-717-1

A PROCESSION OF WORDS

By

Leonard T Coleman

Date of Publication:
December 2002

Published by: Leonard T Coleman

© Copyright Leonard T Coleman

Printed by:
ProPrint
Riverside Cottage
Great North Road
Stibbington
Peterborough PE8 6LR

ISBN: 0-9544144-0-3

CONTENTS

Peter	1
Dull Day	2
When I Am Old	3
Hometown	4
Daydream	5
The Honours Board	6
Thoughts Upon An Inscription	7
Reverie	8
Approach To Christmas	9
Christmas	10
JFK	11
Dunkirk	12
Stalingrad	14
Churchill Lying	15
1953 – Coronation	16
Rain	17
Memories	18
Summer	19
Silver Birch	20
Bomber's Road	21
Maximum Effort	22
Rye – Sussex	25
Winchelsea	26
William Green	27
Brixton	29
Athens	30
Dresden	32
Harry	33
The Toad	36
England In Summer	37
The Shopping Plaza	38
Anthony Aloysius Hancock	40
A Poem A Day	41
Profile	43

PETER

He was so young to die
He never knew the ageing years –
Immortal he.
One of that deathless band they call 'the few,'
Let England mourn her heroes constantly.

Into the air he climbed – on eager wings
Over the places that he used to know
Over the trees – where still a blackbird sings
As we both heard it – not so long ago.

So loving life – he died – without complaining
His sacrifice – shall it be made in vain?
What though our tears continue raining
They cannot bring him back again.

DULL DAY

Dull day – and the heavy-laden sky
Closing in on people and the scene
Taking on a dark and dismal quality
Almost like a thing that is unclean,

Grey Day – and all the brightness hiding,
Nothing but fog, and dreariness of time
Clouds out the sun – that jaded comforter
Drowned – in a sea of mud and mist and slime.

Dark day – that slithers softly into twilight
Slipping away – dissolving into night
Lingering sadly merging into evening
Loath to relinquish just that little light.

WHEN I AM OLD

When I am old, just let them say
'He was a man who went his way,
Trying to share a neighbour's load'
And 'Standing in the narrow road.'

And if there's nothing they can praise
At least I pray – with steady gaze
I can look man full in the face
Knowing that there is no disgrace.

HOMETOWN

I will write tonight of my home town,
If a town it can claim to be,
Where there's peace, and a host of people
Whom I know, and they all know me.

Where the little street smiles a greeting
And I first made my way to school
Where I know I shall find a welcome
Be I beggar, a knave or a fool.

It is there that my thoughts keep returning
Whenever I'm far or forlorn
For where on Earth can a man improve
On the place where he was born?

DAYDREAM

Looking across the valley with the heat-haze shimmering
The sultry greyness of a distant hill,
Man-made windows with the sun's rays glittering,
The lovely Sussex charm – peaceful and still.

Looking across the valley with the
Great orb sinking,
Blazing its last defiance to the day.
Leaning upon a five-barred gate and thinking,
Breathing the fragrance of the new mown hay.

Looking across the valley with the
Night lights gleaming
Softening the shadows – lighting up the sky.
Now is the time for standing and for dreaming –
Dreaming of our love and you and I.

THE HONOURS BOARD IN THE GREAT HALL AT THE SKINNER'S COMPANY'S SCHOOL, TUNBRIDGE WELLS

Yours is the future – guard it well
And by your deeds reflect and amplify
This place, that held us in its magic spell –
A little while until we passed it by.

Yours is the present – all too brief
Although the changes – bell may seem too long
And weary learning futile to your needs
How can your youth-flushed theories be wrong?

Ours is the past – compelling memory
That guides our footsteps still and every scheme,
Lifting the failing, comforting the lonely,
Finding forgotten friendships in the dream.

THOUGHTS UPON AN INSCRIPTION

Engraved upon your shining golden surface
Initials, or a date – perhaps a name
Commemorate this way some passing glory
Some brief incursion to a fleeting fame.

Token perhaps – exchanged or gladly given
Poignant with memory, permeate with love
Warm as the sunshine's sweet and cloying rapture
Shining upon you both from up above.

Lie there – discarded – lost – your fragrance ended
Swift – like a dream when morning gilds the sky
Gone and forgotten that once magic radiance –
vanished –
As every mortal thing must die.

REVERIE

When all my world is hushed and I am gone,
Leaving untold the memories and the dreams,
Then in the misty twilight of beyond
There will unfold so many memories.

There for example I shall know
Just why I came to be, a little while
Reasons for tears, and pain, even for dying
Laughter perhaps – the sweet
Enigma of a smile.

Then – on this speck of sun
This planet – spinning –
This cooling mass – some curious other man
Will struggle out again his little season
And wonder – how it ends – how it began.

APPROACH TO CHRISTMAS!

Approach to Christmas and the dying year
Drags out its span with brittle leafless wood
Along the hedgerows – and the
Bird-song stilled
Except for blackbird's latest noisy brood.

Who knows – perhaps the first faint wisp of snow
Will lightly fall along the naked lane,
Slowly the scene takes on a softer hue
And all the world a fairy land again.

Dim-glowing windows, condensation –
Ringed glimpses of coloured lights and Christmas trees,
Shops with their fluorescent splendour
Catching the eager eye, such things as these.

Packets and parcels bound with coloured paper,
Holly-encrusted cards with
'Just a line to greet you' mumbled, jumbled words –
With furtive thanks exchanged –
And eyes that shine

Parties and gatherings
Around the fireside,
Greeting old friends – the
Season of good cheer –
Bells, paper chains and glittering baubles,
Calendars to greet another coming year.

CHRISTMAS

Christmas – when all the holly-berries glow
And all the world takes on a kinder hue
And that sweet radiance of make believe
Kindles the fires of human kindness too.

Spanning the oceans with its timeless magic,
Softening men's hearts and lighting memories gleams,
So we remember faces half-remembered,
All of our aspirations and our dreams.

Bright glistening lamps upon a window sill,
Tinsel encrusted baubles on a tree,
Faint sounds of music – poignance of reunion –
This is the season as it seems to me.

Laughter of children and their children's children
Bridging the years and banishing the pain
Of other Christmases – we've not forgotten
Links with the past – forged in life's living chain.

JFK – PRESIDENT OF THE UNITED STATES-ASSASSINATED AT DALLAS

Please do not grieve too long my dear
For we would wish to share your tragedy.
We . . . those who never even knew him
Save as an image, maybe, - fleetingly.

And yet we mourn him too, this man, your lover
The father of your children, and your pride,
Who rode to glory on the wheels of greatness
Happy to have you smiling at his side.

God is not mocked – we may not know the secrets
That govern our sweet, brief, and earthly stay,
And that of others whom we love and cherish
The little while we linger on the way.

Take comfort if you can from common people
This was a man the world could not afford to lose
This was a man of principle, and honour,
This was your man – and wisely did you choose.

DUNKIRK

This was our finest hour, upon the beaches
That could have been – and would have been our
                                              own.
But for these sons – these gallant English freemen
Struggling back to help us stand alone.

Dotted like little specks among the sand dunes
Crouching, and cursing each succeeding wave
Stukas! With fiendish song of power – diving
Scattering their deadly missiles on the brave.

This is an army very near disaster
Dazed and out-numbered forced back to the sea
Cruelly opposed – yet who shall say defeated –
Striving to check their dire calamity.

Back to Dunkirk! With all hell's bestial fury
Strafing and driving all along the way
Back to the sea – our dearest oldest ally
Giving us aid to fight another day.

Back to the little ships with gaudy name-plates
And reminiscent names of summers past
Uneasy lulls, historians may call them
Few fleeting years of peace – too good to last.

Wading to cockle-shells amid the thunder
Of guns, and shrieking shrapnel's drenching spray
Through haze of smoke hiding a summer's splendour,
At night the star-shells making it like day.

Back to the harbours, back to English firesides
Weary – unshaven – soaked with flying foam
Sad in their hearts – their mission uncompleted
Yet happy too, our army to be home.

STALINGRAD – DEFEAT OF THE GERMAN ARMY UNDER VON PAULUS

Beside the Volga – gleaming in the moonlight
That river – always fraught with destiny,
A million men are locked in mortal combat
So this once lovely city may be free.

A miracle before a world that wonders
As Hitler's hordes attempting to pass by
Hurl all hell's fury at these noble peasants
Who shame mankind – and teach them how to die.

We give our oath, that with our friends united
These heroes deeds shall not have been in vain
But pass on lips of men down through the ages
Till shell-torn Stalingrad shall rise again.

This is our pledge, take heart you gallant warriors
Proud patriots, force and hate cannot subdue
This world of ours will centuries remember
Stalingrad's name if not the names of you.

In every land when freedom is triumphant
And once again the Volga placid flows
With reverent hush your story will be spoken
Of Stalingrad – eternal as the snows.

CHURCHILL LYING IN STATE IN WESTMINSTER HALL

So the old warrior sleeps and puts away his sword
And freedom's lamp sputters a little at its flame
The lamp he lit . . . around the universe
In every land that loved or feared his name.

Hushed is the world that hushed at each oration
Shuddered – and raised again it's weary head
Spurred to resolve – beyond all resolution
Can it be true? – That mighty heart is dead?

Let us not speak of death for one so mortal
And yet . . . 'Immortal' . . .in the hearts of men
And on their lips, and in their lives, . . . undying
Death you are cheated . . . He is born again.

1953 – CORONATION

Salute we now our lady
Gracious – vivacious, gay
May all our thoughts go out to her
On Coronation day.

Queen of this lovely homeland
Blessed by so many charms
We will defend her cause to the end
Secure from all alarms.

God grant her strength to serve us
Many long years from now
Humbly we pray for her on this day
Remembering her vow.

Charge then your glasses, townsmen!
And on the village green
The toast shall be 'Elizabeth'
'Long may she reign' – our Queen.

RAIN

And the rain came down, silently
Excepting that soft swish and gusty gurgle
As gutters, drains, and culverts run to overflow
Coursing its twisting track to fields below.

Shiny soaked surfaces reflecting brightly
Each temporary lightness of a leaden sky
Splashing from trees, and wheels, and spattering over
The feet of hurrying passers-by.

Rivers and rivulets, mushrooming
Rushing their brief and headlong busy way
Along each roadside ditch and gully
Finding at last some hidden soakaway.

Filling the lakes and ponds where fishes rising
Proclaim the natural order yet again
Hastening to speed mere mortals tardy welcome
Of this refreshing – drenching – shower of rain.

MEMORIES

Memories are sweet and all time is our destiny
Yesterday's dream, today, tomorrow's yearning
Life with its ever-present hopes
Points to the moral – always we are learning.

What is the purpose of each smile and laughter?
How can we know the reason each tear starts?
Time rushes on inexorable – as – ever –
Swift inflexible
Just as we knew it would deep in our hearts.

Knowing all this – we are the human mystery
That God created animal and yet divine
Gives but a hint of final purpose meant us
And the ending
Rests not with us alone – the great design.

SUMMER

Summer – the warm sun glows its July radiance
Lazy bees droning in the heavy air,
Flowers, butterflies, and sleepy hedgehogs,
Colour in profusion everywhere.

Twilight begins to steal the August thunder,
Chiller the dawn that augurs each new day.
Summer – thus ushered in – a blaze of glory,
Daily but surely – starts to slip away.

Nights cool, days shorten and the sky
Takes on a cooler hue;
Mornings darken, meadows glisten,
With such an overdose of dew.

Trees wither, leaves quiver, and the
Thin wind slivers round the bough,
Flowers drooping, heads stooping
Heralds autumn – almost with us now.

SILVER BIRCH

Through the window
There is a birch tree
Silver and slender – rippling in the breeze
Solemnly bending – with its unending
Soft slow swishing symphony.

Standing before me
Like some young maiden
Pure and unsullied, graceful as a swan
Movement perpetual – calmly unhurried
Gently, the birch tree murmurs on.

BOMBER'S ROAD

From the mist of the runway's end
They start their lumbering, tearing run,
Din of engines – rising clamour –
Soaring steadily one by one.

Silhouettes in an evening sky
Roaring their ponderous battle drone
Circling slowly and climbing high
Setting course and then they are gone.

Bearing the men of a lovely land
Brave – with the fearlessness of youth
Riding the clouds on a desperate errand
Staking all in the cause of truth.

MAXIMUM EFFORT (RAF) (OPERATIONAL MISSION OF UTMOST IMPORTANCE)

Maximum effort – magic words
Passing from lip to lip 'along the vine'
With speculation filling in the blanks
That help to start each teller, 'Shoot the line.'

Checks on the bomb types – fuelling plan
Widening the rumours spread – already rife
And what 'Old Baldy' heard his gunner say
The gunnery officer told 'The Groupie's' wife.

Surely not Hamburg? – not again
The armourers say 'there's no incendiary load.'
Berlin . . . perhaps? . . . That's what they think
The Lewis gunners over by the road.

'Heard it from Chiefie – its Cologne'
'That engine-change is wanted on the dot'
'How about J' – 'You bet your life'
'And M for Mother too – the dual – the lot.'

Soon they'll be coming – straggling out
And 'binding' us for early NFT's
Here comes the crewbus now – round 'the perim'
Come on then! 'Fingers out' get off your knees.

'How is the weather?' – 'Not too good'
The mist along the fen land 'will it clamp?'
'What time is take-off?' – 'will they scrub?'
'Maybe they'll land us at some other camp.'

'Waiting a lifetime on the base it seems
Until grotesque the crew again appear –
Bulky and leathered anonymities
As time for take-off gradually creeps near.

Spluttering engines – fitters oaths
And muttered jibes – like-
'Cockpit trouble mate?'
'Prime it once more' – 'Turn the
Port inboard over' and ' just
Our luck to send the bastard late.'

Thunderous roaring – final checks
Maximum boost and then the tearing run
Rising like great black birds malevolent!
Turning on course across the setting sun.

Blissful the silence – darkening sky
All of our eagles winging on their trip
Clutched to their bellies – yellow
Bombs, to shower down
'Cry havoc and let slip.'

Now it is over – anticlimax –
Waiting begins again – and NAAFI tea
Pondering that early dawn of resurrection –
Brief hours away
Shattering our reverie.

'When will they be back?' – fleeting shadows
Lumbering and looming in the early light
How many shadows? – 'Here's J for Johnnie'
Some of our shadows may not
Last the night.

Home again gladly – misty vapours
Trailing around 'The trestles' and 'The ACC'
Broad grins of welcome – 'Did you have a picnic?'
'Piece of cake cobber' – 'But that flak !!'

Intelligence questions – never ending
'What did it look like?' – 'Mass of flaming red'
Weary rejoinders – 'Course we found the target'
'Hurry up sir – and let's all get to bed!'

So for a respite – welcome – fleeting
Until the 'Magic words' are heard again
Glow in the east – the sun's already rising
Mournful – the whistle of an early train.

Glossary

Cockpit trouble: pilot error
The Perim: a/o perimeter road
Chiefie: Flt/Sgt
Scrub: to abandon a raid
Groupies wife: G/Captain's wife
'Along the vine': rumour (the grapevine)
Clamp: a sudden fenland fog
'Shoot the line': airmen's gossip
NFT's: night flying tests
Trestles and the ACC: A/field equipment including starter accumulator

RYE – SUSSEX

Rye, that lowly Sussex fortress
Born of truly British cast,
Lies serene amid the marshes
Lingering on its famous past.

Down one of its little side streets
Still there ticks a solemn clock
Bearing on its dial a motto
Seeming cynically to mock:

'Time is as a shadow passing'
Is the gist of that old text –
As we look around we wonder
Where it's shadow passeth next.

Time has brought its change upon Rye
Her once greatness turned to nought
Taken from her that great glory
Which her founding fathers bought.

WINCHELSEA

Up a hill long steep and winding
Through an arch of bygone years
Round the corner, by the look-out
Winchelsea village now appears.

Quaint with little cobbled sidewalks,
Crazy buildings old and worn,
Painted windows in the church
That stands amid a sea of lawn.

In the background stands a windmill,
Stripped of sail and soaked with rot,
Watching Winchelsea like parent
Hovering by her infant's cot.

In the distance – to the southward –
Gleam the strips of blue and white
From the ancient look out glittering
As the wave-tops catch the light.

From behind the cliff the moon peeps
Shining its pale yellow glow
Softly comes the sound of music
From some nearby bungalow.

So we leave the village sleeping,
Down the winding hill again,
Silence over dyke and marshland
Save the whistling of a mournful train.

WILLIAM GREEN

William Green was only ten
And yet he always knew just when
To smile and say 'Good morning'
To the people that he met and knew.

He always tried to be polite
He raised his cap and said 'Good night'
And when old ladies from his road
Went shopping – he would share the load.

At parties he would never grab
The largest bun – the biggest slab
He never tried to jump the queue
When local buses came in view.

He washed his face and combed his hair,
At strangers he would never stare,
And when each day he went to school
He cleaned his boots – well, as a rule.

And yet with all the gifts he had
At lessons he was very bad,
The teachers nearly tore their hair
And ceased their efforts in despair.

The other boys won scholarships
And went with satchels on their hips,
But William tried with no avail –
It seemed that he was bound to fail.

One day an old professor trying
To climb some steps, found William crying
And on enquiry of the lad
Discovered what had made him sad.

Then William lent a helping hand
The old man smiled and said that's grand
'Pass your exams' – 'Some people never'
'There's other ways of being clever.'

'So don't forget – the golden rule
Is not the way you shine at school'
'Keep trying through – perhaps you will'
But sentiment is more than skill.

BRIXTON

The Brixton that I knew in 1937
Is gone forever, and I know
You cannot turn the clock back on nostalgia
And regulate it so that it runs slow.

A happy place it was as I remember
Brixton Astoria – Electric Avenue
The darkened street that market stalls enlivened
By flickering lights of fizzling gas turned low.

At Christmas time the eager children's faces
Pressed to the glass – reflecting Colliers store
The holly wreaths, the mistletoe, and home-made sweets
The dazzling glitter – and the endless poor.

Is it so different – the scene so altered
The eager faces – lined from long ago,
Still there – but faltering a little
With steps unsure and wavering and slow.

Today the same kaleidoscope unfolding
Yet coloured – with a wider spectrum view
The children's faces – many different cultured
The aged – foreboding have their problems too.

The Brixton that I hope for in the future
With tolerance, kindness, hope, integrity
The good times and the bad now intermingled
Combining all that precious memory.

ATHENS

Athens – my lovely ancient city
Though some decry you and dispute your worth
With talk of smog and traffic snarled-up sidewalks
But still for me – a magic place on Earth.

Arrive by plane in bustling Glyfada
And glimpse the junk-filled yards along the way
To your hotel – you may begin to wonder
What place is this – where I have come to stay?

But breathe the warm night-breeze before your
                                                  judgement
The fragrance of the wild-thyme perfumed air
That blows from off the heath around Hymettus
And filters into near Syntagma Square.

Acropolis – its stone-encrusted splendour
Majestic – Parthenon and Hadrians Gate
Temple of Zeus – wander through the ruins
Of long ago – and contemplate their fate.

Or stand amid the modern concrete jungle
That sprawls around at Lycabettus feet
That tiny mountain rising – sheer – incongruous
Spilling its feet into the city street.

Or ride its old funicular to stardom
All glittering in the Athens purple night
Then gaze across the roof-tops to Piraeus
A mile away across a blaze of light.

The mighty roar of traffic – never ending
Snaking its journey seven-wide to town
Along your one-way streets that seem unbending
By German architects designed – of great renown.

Botanic gardens green well-watered splendour
Beside the palace walls – emblazoned crest
A flame that flickers – sentinel – and evzones
Guarding the spot the unknown soldier rests.

So may he rest in peace in this fair city
In this place where democracy was spawned
And struggled through a thousand different ages
Until the day civilisation dawned.

DRESDEN

Why weep for Dresden – yes it was a sin
But war is sin – and ever since the world began
The testimony grows – the legend born –
Man's inhumanity to other man.

What matters where the bombs cascading fall
Destroy – decapitate – and maim and slay –
The message that they bring is just the same,
Merely degree of devastation and decay.

The living weep – among the debris strewn
Their life-long work crumbled beneath their feet
Rubble – encrusted evidence
Of every shattered broken little street.

Was it so different then in Whitechapel?
Were Stratford, Plaistow, not so sacrosanct?
Was Coventry a different sort of place then?
With life there valued less – or maybe scant.

No! only hypocrites bear evidence
To try to justify such feeble ends
For war is futile and we know it causes havoc
And can make enemies of friends.

Missiles discriminate but little as they fall
Among the innocent as well as foes
But that is how it is – and always has been
Or so I understand the story goes.

HARRY, THE STORY OF A STRAY CAT

Harry was a cat – an elegant cat
And Burmese – so I've recently been told –
Describing him you note I use the past tense
For reasons I shall presently unfold.

He came to us at Christmas I recall it
As we sat gazing after lunch we saw
His shadowed shape outlined against the snow line
He touched the patio glass with seal-point paw.

A timid cat – at first he ran away
But tempting him with turkey we were able
Eventually, as hunger overcame him
Persuasively – to coax him to our table.

By afternoon he'd wandered off – forlornly
And that was what we thought – we were mistaken,
On Boxing Day he reappeared to greet us
Beneath the garage door he crawled snow-shaken.

Some friends who came to tea thought that they knew him
'I'm sure he's from the house across the way'
One said – They have a lot of cats
And notices – beware of dogs – they say.

The nights were cold that winter – I remember
The hard frosts biting in the ground
But every morning – when I got the car out
I noticed Harry – sleeping snug and sound.

He obviously had quite usurped our garage
And seemed to like his new adopted home
But conscience pricked – eventually my wife said
He's not ours – you must take him home.

And so it was I finally decided
To brave the dogs – so mindful of my fate
Strolled down the lane with Harry but my luck held
The owner stood outside his garden gate.

'Is this your cat?' I queried when I saw him
'Why yes, that's Harry,' he at once replied,
'We called him 'Dirty Harry' when they found him,
This gang of kids who brought him here inside.'

'You see we lost a Siamese of value
And advertised within the local news
The children obviously thought they'd found him
Especially when they heard his plaintive mews.'

'He seemed to be a wanderer although valued
But not our cat – he's just another stray
We had no heart to disillusion children
So paid them the reward and let him stay.

'But he's not dirty really by his nature
He's clean – affectionate – and loves to play
My wife is very keen on him and loves him
But try her best – she cannot make him stay.

'We had hoped when we moved here he would settle
He doesn't like the Dobermans – although
We thought with other cats he would be happy
But he's a loner – and is not you know.'

And so it was increasingly apparent
That Harry liked us too – and shared our home
We both became so fond of him and loved him
As last he seemed to lose the urge to roam.

Our wood was like a paradise for Harry
No other cats – and not a sign of dogs
He climbed the trees and sunned himself and gambolled
And chased the squirrels round the piles of logs.

I often used to take him home at evening
But he'd be back – as large as life next day.
No matter what they tried they couldn't hold him
He simply never had the wish to stay.

Until the man collected him one morning
We well recall that sad and awful day
'Is Harry there – why yes – I'll go and fetch him
We've sold our house – we're moving out today.'

My wife and I are desolate and wonder
If Harry will survive his new-found fence
So now you understand my early problem
If Harry is or was – explains the tense.

THE TOAD

No thing of beauty you may think
Yet agile in retreat.
Painfully but surely traversing
The tiny stones spurned by your feet.

It turns away and slides beneath
A moss encrusted stone
Where it will sleep and hibernate
Unfettered and alone.

The gardeners friend its diet sparse
Of insect fly and slug.
He welcomes it among the grass
Or in his favourite trug.

Will carry it to some safe haven
Where released it can
Continue its mud – earthly role
And it's nocturnal span.

Not all God's creatures beautiful
In wisdom made them all
But part of his great universe
All creatures great and small.

ENGLAND IN SUMMER

The splendour of a lovely English summer
Pure white soft cumulus set in the blue,
Green grass that is the hallmark of our England
Foreground or background to its every view.

The sweetness of the early Chiltern landscape,
A silver ribboned river sliding by.
The tree – the distant purple of the hillsides
The vastness of the never ending sky.

The leaping salmon climbing to its spawning
Among the rock-strewn rapids of the Wye
That twists its course, elaborate discerning
Making a picture pleasing to the eye.

Is there a land so testament to beauty
So paramount with simple rural charm
With woodland walks that fade into horizon
Or terminate at some old fashioned farm?

No there is not – for I have travelled widely
Seen Athens, Paris, Auckland even Rome.
Their myriad charms each in its way breathtaking
Do not compare my friend – for this is home.

THE SHOPPING PLAZA

You've seen them – nearly every city has one
Or any place that calls itself a town.
The culmination of some planner's nightmare,
A massive monument to trading – down.

A vast great area – internal car parks
Eternal shadows too – each dark-spilled room.
With shining fluorescents to illumine
The inky depths of claustrophobic gloom.

Through swinging doors into another universe
With iron railing pineapple gold tipped.
Vast concourses of gilt victoriana
To which it seems our old/new world has slipped.

Crowded the elevators and the stairway
With all editions of the human race.
The rising/falling lifts that loft you skywards
Or downward to some pre-determined place.

Do you want trousers, jeans or merely dusters?
Here you will find them catalogued with all
The other things you need for basic living.
All congregate in one vast shopping mall.

A shining place of pools and glittering fountains
A fairy tale of human gotten gains.
Protected at vast cost from all the elements in brightness –
For of course it never rains.

Is this for you – for you your whole life fashioned,
The governance that rules your earthly stay?
Or are you secretly enamoured
Of life as lived before, a simpler way?

An old world teashop near the great cathedral,
That monument to other famous years.
With little shops that cluster in the high street
And hand to mouth trade-out their inner fears.

Is this the pattern then for future yearning
All electronic all embracing span?
Where television rules our every craving
Stifling emotion and our fellow man?

So think of these things in the shopping plaza
(For which I'm sure I'd never get to rhyme)
That maybe it's a place to go and linger
And shop a little – but not all the time.

ANTHONY ALOYSIUS HANCOCK

Anthony Aloysius Hancock was his name
In distant land he died – sad and alone –
And so I contemplate this complex man
Who tugged my soul – and claimed it for his own.

Of all his virtues – one we know so well
He stood alone – his timing skill unique
For stand up comedy is hard to sell
From smiling lips when life can be so bleak.

His striving for perfection made him slave
To gain his laughs from ordinary folks,
Driving ambition to an early grave
To stimulate his endless flow of jokes.

Well we remember him, his mobile face
His phrases, quips, his shrill outrageous shout
'I thought my mother couldn't really cook,
At least her gravy used to move about!'

And so I mourn him – and indeed my loss
Is shared I know by many of his friends,
Thank God we have his videos and tapes
Although of course they cannot make amends.

Like Anthony of old – who craved the ears
Of Ancient Rome – a master of his art,
A prey to all those fragile earthly fears
And jesting with his lips but not his heart.

Let us salute him – Anthony the man
Who made us laugh – and countered many a frown,
Let this then be his famous epitaph
'If not to this a great man – to this a great clown.'

A POEM A DAY

A Poem a day should be a worthy cause
To write one's thoughts upon a virgin page
A flow of words – with scarce the time for pause
Each little strutting on our mortal stage.

Our hopes, ambitions, fears, our daily routine
Dull, common place, world shattering or merely bland,
Ring out, reverberate with glamour lutine
Like Lloyd's Insurance bell throughout the land.

Dear Reader – judge us not too trivial scribbler
Flotsam and jetsam of another's schemes
Think on your own aspiring loves and prejudices,
All of your yearning visions and your dreams.

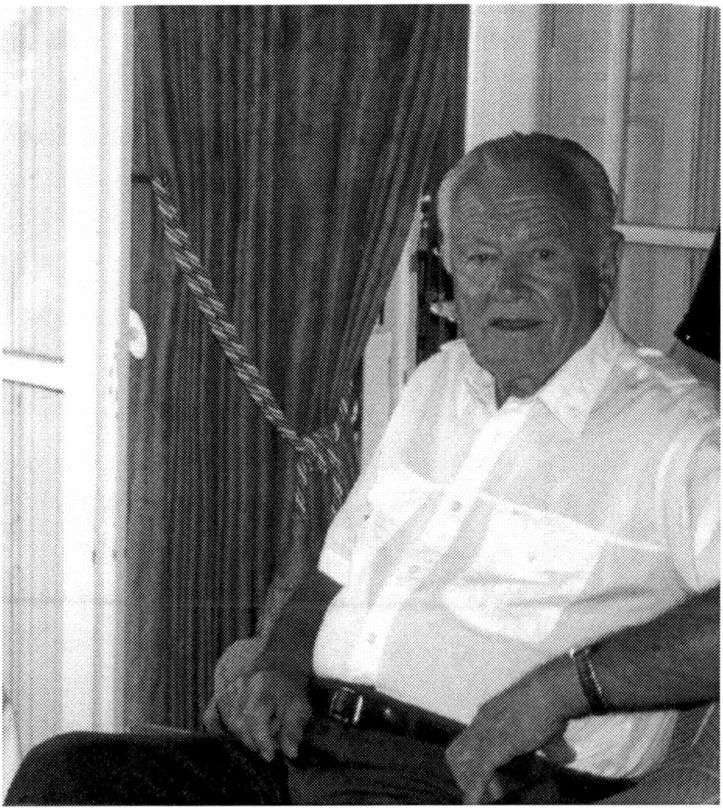

PROFILE

I was born in Frant, Sussex and was educated at the local village school, and then at the Skinners Company's School, Tunbridge Wells. I worked in a Watchmakers and Jewellers shop, and then in Local Government. During World War II, I served in the Royal Air Force as a technician, and although I never flew operationally I flew many hours on air tests on Auto Controls, Bombsights and General Instruments as an NCO. I returned to work in Local Government until 1978 as a Senior Committee Clerk and was awarded the Queen's Silver Jubilee Medal in 1997 for long service. My first wife died in 1963 and I am married again very happily to my present wife, Pam, who has recently retired as a secretary/PA to the Chief Executive of a large group of companies. For many years I played in dance bands in and around the Medway towns and Sussex, first on trumpet and then on saxophone and clarinet. I also have played piano and even drums on occasion, but nowadays only for my own amusement as a hobby, together with my poetry which has been published quite a lot in the Spotlight Series and anthologies by Forward Press etc. I live in West Sussex and like to write about nature and rural subjects with the occasional biography or items of topical interest.